A RANDOM HOUSE BOOK published by Random House New Zealand
18 Poland Road, Glenfield, Auckland, New Zealand

For more information about our titles go to www.randomhouse.co.nz

A catalogue record for this book is available from the National Library of New Zealand

Random House International, Random House, 20 Vauxhall Bridge Road, London,
SW1V 2SA, United Kingdom; **Random House Australia Pty Ltd,** Level 3, 100 Pacific
Highway, North Sydney 2060, Australia; **Random House South Africa Pty Ltd,**
Isle of Houghton, Corner Boundary Road and Carse O'Gowrie, Houghton 2198,
South Africa; **Random House Publishers India Private Ltd,** 301 World Trade Tower,
Hotel Intercontinental Grand Complex, Barakhamba Lane, New Delhi 110 001, India

First published 2008. Reprinted 2008 (twice). Reprinted 2009 (twice). Reprinted 2010. Reprinted 2011.

© 2008 Justin Brown

The moral rights of the author have been asserted

ISBN 978 1 86979 022 6

'How Bizarre' (Jansson/Fuemana) © Universal Music Publishing Pty Ltd. All rights
reserved. International copyright secured. Reprinted with permission. 'Cheryl Moana
Marie' (Kipner/Bowles) © Universal/MCA Music Publishing Pty Ltd. All rights
reserved. International copyright secured. Reprinted with permission. 'Ten Guitars'
(Mills) © Valley Music Ltd. administered by Universal/MCA Music Publishing Pty
Ltd. All rights reserved. International copyright secured. Reprinted with permission.
'Dominion Road' Words and music by Don McGlashan. 'There is No Depression in
New Zealand' Words: Richard von Sturmer. Music: Don McGlashan. Published by
Native Tongue Music Publishing Ltd. Reprinted with permission.

Design: Trevor Newman

Printed by South China Printing Co. Ltd.

KIWI SPEAK

Justin Brown

RANDOM HOUSE
NEW ZEALAND

INTRODUCTION 7

1 CLASSIC KIWI SPEAK 8

2 MUM SPEAK 26

3 DAD SPEAK 38

4 NANA SPEAK 52

5 TV SPEAK 62

6 SHOWER SPEAK 78

7 FARM SPEAK 86

8 SCHOOL SPEAK 98

CONTENTS

9 RETRO SCHOOL SPEAK 108

10 SATURDAY SPORTS SPEAK 116

11 HORSE-RACING SPEAK 126

12 PUB SPEAK 134

13 STROPPY SPEAK 144

14 ROAD-RAGE SPEAK 154

15 STREET SPEAK 162

16 THINGS YOU'LL NEVER
HEAR A SELF-RESPECTING
KIWI MALE SAY 168

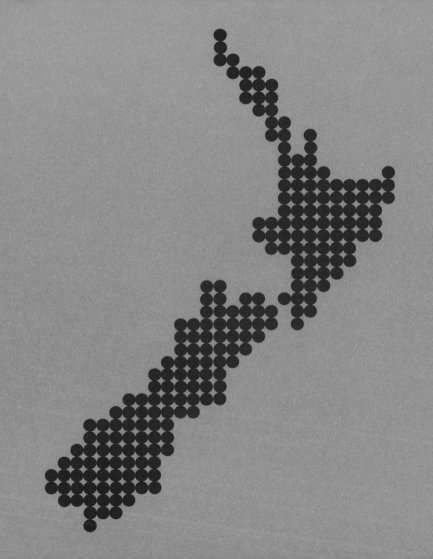

Introduction

New Zealand was the first country to see the sun and give women the vote. It's also the only place on Earth where builders eat pie sandwiches for lunch. This land of plenty invented the jetboat, spreadable butter and the electric fence. It's also the only place where jandals and shorts are considered 'semi-formal'. Aotearoa boasts more bookshops and golf courses per capita than any other country. It's also the only land where you can say 'bugger' without getting in trouble. Welcome to *Kiwi Speak*, a book that toasts the way New Zealanders yarn. There are sayings we used to say. There are sayings we shouldn't say. There are put-downs, pick-me-ups and things you can yell in the pub. You'll discover how Kiwis lose their rag on the road, in the bach and up over the backblocks. The little toerags have their own lingo too. (When they're not wagging, that is.)

Maybe you're new to New Zealand. Maybe it fits like an old pair of Stubbies. Whatever the reason, why not pull on your ug boots, jump in the La-Z-Boy, grab an L&P and check out a few of these beauties. Oh, and don't sweat it if you're not a big reader — you'll knock this bastard off in no time. PS: Though these sayings aren't all exclusive to New Zealand, they are used in everyday speech, often having been passed down generations. Some youngsters born after Helen started running the joint won't know some of the old ones. Conversely, your nana probably reckons the 'Street Speak' section sounds as ludicrous as fart tax. One thing's for sure, New Zealanders, we're different. So let's have a shandy and celebrate.

CLASSIC
KIWI
SPEAK

From the dairy to the beach to the hangi — in fact anywhere you find Kiwis — you'll find the following crackers being used. If you're from out of town, however, and you want to make them sound real authentic, do as most Kiwis do: drop a few vowels here and there, and raise the intonation at the end of each word as if you're asking a question.

A few examples: A-medgen (as in the title of the John Lennon song) going straight to 'bid' (what you sleep on) after scoffing all those 'fush and chups' (shark and tatties). Remember, too, if Dr Seuss was a Kiwi his most famous book would be titled *The Cet in the Het*.

In any case, before we get too carried away and go arse over tit, grab your cuz and have a gawk at the grouse words of wisdom that follow. You'll have it sussed in no time, hunky dory, sweet as, home 'n' hosed.

As we say around here, 'Kick it in the guts, Trev!'

'How ya garn?'

Kiwis are right into shortening things: jail terms and odds on Bledisloe Cup matches spring to mind. Alas, it's no different with words. After all, why waste your time with, 'Good day, fine sir, how would you be going on this splendiferous morning?' when you could just get away with the above?

'Good as gold.'

As in: 'How's the job?' 'Good as gold.'
Meaning the employment in question is as good as having gold in your pocket. In the old days having gold, as opposed to paper money, meant you could exchange it for goods and services anywhere.

'Ka pai!'

Maori for 'good'. Even your average Palagi or Honky feels confident enough using the above. Indeed some, the daring and reckless Pakeha, even attempt to place it in a full sentence: 'Ka pai kai (food) in my puku (belly).'

'Haven't seen you in yonks!'

A cracker of a word, yonks. Literally meaning 'ages', one theory is that it comes from donkey's years, another is that it's taken from years, months and weeks.

'She'll be right!'

Arguably the most popular Kiwi phrase of all time. Can be used in response to a number of enquiries: 'Shall we lock the car?'; 'Do we have enough petrol to get us to Blenheim?'; 'Are you wearing a condom?'

'You can't handle the jandal!'

I only recently learnt that the common Kiwi jandal got its name from a contraction of 'Japanese sandal'. The above would have been perfect in a New Zealand version of *A Few Good Men*:
'You can't handle . . . the jandal!'

'He's a kumara short of a hangi.'

The lights are on but nobody's home. His elevator doesn't go to the top. Dumber than a box of rocks. Not playing with a full deck. If you don't get my drift by now, you obviously don't have both oars in the water.

'Ya reckon?'

Typical response to your best friend's admission to having the hots for the guy from accounts who everyone else thinks is a complete bogan.

'I'm going to see a man about a dog.'

More often than not this saying comes out of the Kiwi male's mouth. And it has many meanings: 'I'm going trout fishing'; 'The pokies are calling my name'; 'Must get that boat I've always promised myself'.

'Sweet as.'

As Kiwi as a potato-top pie, a box of Jaffas, or a game of Swingball. Literally translates to 'yes', or 'agreed'. 'F***ing A' or 'Right as rain' can also be used.

'Yeah . . . nah.'

Likely response from a New Zealand sports captain when being interviewed post-match, as in, 'Yeah . . . nah, the game was ours for the taking but we just couldn't put the final nail in the coffin.' 'So does this mean retirement for you as captain?' 'Yeah . . . nah . . . yeah . . . nah.' Clear as mud.

'Good on ya.'

Not a good one to send by text, as it can be taken two ways. 'Good on ya,' as in, 'I'm stoked for you, well done.' Alternatively, 'Oh, good on ya', as in, 'Thanks for spilling Coke all over my new boardies!'

'She's a bit of a dag.'

The woman in question, who has come to a Kiwi-themed party dressed as Peter Plumley-Walker (true story!), is a bit of a 'hard case', comedian, or joker. (Plumley-Walker was a cricket umpire who famously died during a bondage and discipline session in 1989 and whose still-bound body was turfed over Huka Falls.)

'No wucking furries.'

A classic piece of Kiwi Speak that can even be used in front of a toddler. Not dissimilar to the well-worn term 'She had a cunning array of stunts.'

'Piece of piss, mate.'

See above.

'GO-ORNE, be a sport!'

Used by the bludger who's doing his best to scrounge your last potato fritter.

'Geez, I busted a gut.'

To make an intense effort by mowing the lawn, trimming the hedges and cleaning the gutters. Normally, it must be said, because you stumbled in at 4am and slept in your mother-in-law's bathroom.

'Cheerio.'

How a kids' party sausage ever became a way of saying goodbye in New Zealand is anyone's guess. 'Cherry' is also used, as is 'Ta ta!'

'Na night.'

On *The Waltons* it was 'Good night, John-Boy.' In New Zealand, once again, abbreviation is the key.

'What are ya?'

A Kiwi's way of saying, 'Is that all you've got?'
The most effective reply, as I discovered in primary school, is 'What are *you*?'

'He's on a cushy number.'

The employee in question works four-hour days, gets a company car, overseas trips, an expense account, client lunches and front-row seats to big gigs. Yes, the person in question *is* hated — but by God they're happy!

'Don't be such a spazz.'

A typical Kiwi sister's response to her brother for being, well, her brother. Trust me, I know all about this.

'She's built like a brick shithouse.'

A good Kiwi to have on your side should you be on the receiving end of a knuckle sandwich.

'It was a bloody mish all right!'

In other words: 'My three-year-old could have given better directions!' ('Mish' being short for 'mission'.)

'Up at sparrow's fart, gotta drive to Parther's Arse.'

When Kiwi kids find out they're allowed to say 'Whakapapa' without getting into trouble, they think all their Christmases have come at once. One good thing about being an adult, apart from being allowed to stay up for all of *Outrageous Fortune*, is calling the place name Arthur's Pass the above.

'Bring round half a doz and we'll make a night of it.'

The best parties are unplanned, which explains why so many people are let down on New Year's Eve. The six beers, as mentioned above, won't exactly set the world on fire but when a Kiwi says 'make a night of it' you may as well pack the *SingStar* and leave the car at home.

'They'll charge you an arm and a leg.'

Buying Bluff oysters in Auckland is not for the faint-hearted. Indeed, chucking in the job, moving to Southland and setting up a fishing charter would be far more affordable. Not to mention fun.

'Where's the dunny?'

Translation: 'Could you show me the way to the washroom please?'
Other Kiwi names for the little boys' room:
'long drop', 'bog', 'shitter', 'lav' and 'loo'.

'What's for pud?'

Translation: 'Will there be a sweet treat following the main course?'
Response: 'Yeah, if you get up and make it!'

'Spot on!'

Absolutely correct. Exactly right. 100 per cent.
Inspired a kids' TV show of the same name.

'Rough as guts.'

This Kiwi isn't averse to getting his hands dirty or afraid of a little bit of hard work. Alternatively, it can also mean the New Zealander in question fell out of the ugly tree and hit every branch on the way down. You get the idea.

'Can't come in, boss. Got the dreaded lurgy.'

There's a fine art to 'wagging' or 'throwing a sickie', though telling all and sundry that you have bird flu or Ebola will normally do it. The above is slang for something less serious but more catching. Not to mention honest!

'Righto, give it heaps!'

Typically muttered to your best mate who has bought, against everyone's advice, the worst car in the country. Alas, the next couple of minutes won't be pretty; best to block the kids' ears unless you want them to hear the epitome of profanity.

'Wrap your laughing gear around that one.'

First mastered by the irreverent Barry Crump who, when not driving poor old Scotty to drink in the Toyota ads in 1982, was taking his ute up tracks only bovine should use.

'Up shit creek in leaky gumboots.'
'Up the boohai shooting pukekos with a popgun.'

Whenever the New Zealand cricket team play a test against Australia, they inevitably lose more wickets than they make runs. The above sayings should cover how the average fan feels knowing that the five-day match will be finished in two.

'I wasn't born yesterday.'

Likely reply to, 'I heard they took the word "gullible" out of the dictionary.' Even more colloquial is the sarcastic yet extremely effective, 'Yeah right!'

'I'm just yanking your chain.'

'I'm pulling your leg! The All Blacks didn't *really* lose the quarter final against France. But don't watch the replay, it's boring . . . hey, look over there!'

Kiwi mums are a wonderful breed. They're smart, spunky and possess a don't-mess-with-me attitude. They're magicians too, able to produce an unending supply of Pineapple Lumps and lemonade Popsicles should the need arise. (Or if they need a really good bribe.)

Even though they're knackered from a day's work, they still find the time to make Marmite on toast and hot Milo when you return from school. The Kiwi mum is there when your bunny dies. And she watches Idol with you even though she'd rather be watching Coro. She is the Queen of Feigning Enthusiasm when, in reality, she'd far prefer a glass of wine and a chat on the phone (uninterrupted!).

'It's puckarooed!'

The dishwasher in question is buggered, stuffed or — another classic Kiwi term — completely had it. Puckarooed is actually a corruption of the Maori word 'pakaru', meaning 'broken' or 'ruined'. Either way, it won't change the fact that the only decision you'll be making in the next five minutes is whether you'll be washing or drying.

'Do you want a clip around the ear?'

Normally muttered when the said Kiwi mum has discovered Double Happies and Tom Thumbs in her child's school bag.

'If everyone else jumped off the Harbour Bridge, would you?'

An adventurous Kiwi kid is surely the wrong person to ask, 'If everyone else jumped in the Avon, would you?' 'Hell, yeah, what time?'

'What's the magic word?'

Every family has their own magic word — 'please', 'abracadabra', and 'hocus pocus' seem to do the trick — though there are a few Kiwi kids who take their cue from the *The Addams Family* movies: 'What's the magic word?' 'NOW!'

'Don't pea on the table.'

Now that I'm a parent I know how easy it is to use the same jokes over and over. The above was my mother's Achilles heel, always used when the said lone vegetable rolled next to the bowl of mashed spuds.

'Shall I put the "spew-mante" in the fridge?'

Kiwi mums like a bottle of Bernadino because it's cheap. Kiwi kids prefer cask wine because once it's finished the plastic bladder makes a fantastic football. Miami Wine Cooler used to cop a fair bit of flack but spumante (pronounced 'spew-mante') was, for the obvious reasons, easily the most memorable.

'If you're good, you can have a Jelly Tip.'

Kiwi kids don't realise there is nothing better —
and never will be — than standing on the back lawn, naked,
eating chocolate-covered icecream and jelly on a stick. That's life, right there.

'Marjorie and Bruce are going to the bach for Waitangi Day.'

You wouldn't hear this sentence anywhere else on the planet.
A bach (Kiwi for beach house) is the ultimate retreat on
New Zealand's national day, in the balmy month of February.

'No wonder you're not hungry, you had a 50c mix half an hour ago!'

Once upon a time a bag of lollies was the size of your hand.
They lasted for weeks. And you could never eat all your tea. Oh well . . .

'Sharon's moving to the wop wops.'

Otherwise known as the 'boonies', the wop wops are literally back and beyond:
no broadband; no neighbours; no cops. (You didn't hear that last bit from me.)

'A boy in Wanganui had his eye out with a rubber band.'

Regardless of the dangerous activity, the boy in Wanganui with the bad aim was always used as an example. Alas, it never worked, with most kids willing to lose a body part if it meant they could maim their sibling.

'Any more backchat and you won't be going to the blue-light disco.'

The blue-light disco was a dance put on by the police. It was a place where 12-year-old boys wished they could hug the girls when they danced, instead of the walls. Hormones, testosterone, Fanta and Dad (parked 28 blocks away).

'Wait till your father gets home.'

You have to feel for the dad who works all day, endures a heinous traffic jam and is dying for a beer, only to find once he walks in the front door that he has to yell at his kid for feeding crayons to the family axolotl.

'Say ta?'

It would be fine if this was said just the once. Sadly, for first-time parents anyway, it's monotony epitomised: 'Ta? Ta? Ta? Callum, say ta? Ta? Ta? Ta? Callum! Ta! Ta!' This drawn-out manners lesson is typically followed by 'Where have our guests gone?'

'If you eat that now, you'll ruin your dinner.'

The above is likely to be followed with the classic, clichéd, downright obvious, 'When they're gone they're gone!'

'Not tonight, love, I'm had it.'

Bad news for Dad.

'Who won?'

This is normally asked by the Kiwi wife, who had the common sense to go to bed four hours before her sports-mad husband. The surly response is always the same: 'THEM!', which is typically followed by 'It's always them!'

'He, he, one day you'll be prime minister!'

My mum, I'm sure like many others around the country, used to tug on my cheeks while saying the above. Former PM Robert Muldoon had this dent in his face, the joke being if Mum pulled mine long enough, I may one day get to run the country. And ruin it, like Muldoon. That aside, he did have the best comebacks. When a journalist once hassled him for kicking a man when he was down, Piggy replied, 'When better? He, he, he!'

'Hercules Morse as big as a horse, Muffin McLay like a bundle of hay . . .'

'. . . and Hairy Maclary from Donaldson's Dairy.' There wouldn't be many young Kiwi mums who haven't read these lines to their toddlers in bed.

'Who spilt pav on my Edmonds cook book?'

Hot debate continues to rage on who invented the 'pav', the strongest contenders, of course, being the trans-Tasman neighbours.
But Australia stole Phar Lap, Crowded House and Russell Crowe.
We keep the pav! Note: as for the cook book, it's one of the biggest-selling New Zealand books of all time, constantly on the bestseller lists.

'Slip, slop, slap before you go anywhere, mister!'

A health campaign in New Zealand that asked folk to, 'Slip on a shirt, slop on sunscreen and slap on a hat' to prevent skin cancer.

New Zealand dads are one of a kind. The good ones are out there on Saturday mornings taking their kids to sport. The bad ones are still wearing Stubbies. Most Kiwi dads have time for the family, as long as that means having 80 minutes off to watch the rugby. They're proud of their sheds and very protective of their barbecues, not to mention their daughters. They're pedantic at packing the boot on holidays and, once there, are always the first to challenge you at Swingball.

Much like Kiwi mums, dads have a unique way of talking. (Of course, sometimes it takes little more than a look to realise you're in hot water.) For many of these sayings, you have your grandfather to blame. Or your great grandfather. And, before you blokes criticise, just remember that when you become a pedantic packer and Stubbies model you too will be belting them out with reckless abandon.

'Go and ask your mother.'

And the inevitable reply: 'I've already asked her; she said no.'

'Go and ask your mother for a plate for the meat.'

If I had a sausage for every time I heard my dad say this, I'd have the world's biggest casserole. As we all know, you're not to put cooked meat on the plate you brought the raw stuff out on. As a result, dads all over New Zealand request a clean plate upon which to put their culinary — normally 'Cajun' — masterpieces.

'I'm off to the shed, I could be a while.'

It took me a long time to realise why fathers were so in awe of the common garden shed. Now I understand completely. The 'den', 'man-space' or 'cave' is purely an escape from the kids. Example: 'Just going to sweep the shed for the fourth time today, love. By the way, Jack needs a nappy change.'

'Oh, give me a break!'

This is typically heard when the said Kiwi dad's lawnmower has run out of petrol with only a tiny patch of grass left. Or it's muttered when he can't wind that stupid plastic cord to the inside of the weedeater.

'Get in the car, we're leaving!'

This can be used on a number of occasions:
• when you superglue your sister's hands together;
• when you pop the neighbour's waterbed;
• when, upon seeing an obese shopper at the supermarket
checkout, you say, 'Wow, that man has a baby in his tummy!'

'Keep these grades up and you'll be a third-year fifth!'

Being 'held back' in school was embarrassing to a class pet.
To a delinquent it was an honour. But, by jingoes, if Dad found out . . .

'Where's your stack hat?'

Also known as a 'skid lid', bicycle helmets became compulsory
on New Zealand roads in 1994. Our parents have no idea how lucky they were,
never having to wear one!

'Okay, I've got four fish, three potato fritters, one chip and one spring roll.'

What Kiwi dad didn't stand in the lounge with a scrap of paper and a pen taking orders on a Friday night? If you were lucky he'd even take you to the fish and chip shop, where you waited with bated breath for 'number 54 — four fish, three potato flitter, one spling loll and one chip!'

'I'm gonna hit the hay, gotta be up for the dawn parade.'

The dawn parade is the most popular observance of Anzac Day.
It is timed to coincide with the initial landings at Gallipoli on 25 April 1915.
The time is also poignant for veterans who recall the routine dawn 'stand-to'
of their war service. It's an emotional experience and one that
every Kiwi youngster should get out of bed for.

'One more over, then I'll come up to bed.'

An over in cricket is roughly three minutes long, and that's where most Kiwi cricket fans lose the concept of time. One over becomes two, becomes midnight, becomes grumpy Dad come sunrise. It's best to remember that New Zealand teams mostly win when we're asleep.

'I've only got enough time for an Aussie shower.'

Muttered when the said Kiwi dad has been chopping bamboo all afternoon and doesn't have time for a shit, shower and shave before going out for tea. Thank God for Brut 33 and Old Spice!

'Did you wet the bed?'

Typically said to the Kiwi kid who is up before the rest of the household on a school morning.

'She went mad so I shot her.'

A Kiwi dad's response to the overused, not to mention downright annoying, 'Where's Mum?'

'Wait till your mother gets home!'

See similar entry in Mum Speak.

'I could make that.'

Kiwi dads are a resourceful bunch. Indeed, if one sees an elaborate piece of art made out of nothing but chicken wire, garden rakes and pantyhose, he drives home straight away to make it.

'If you clean your rugby boots you can have a Hundreds and Thousands sandwich.'

Otherwise known as 'fairy bread' (though not to boys!), you can't beat Hundreds and Thousands on fresh white bread with butter. Almost worth tidying your room for.

'Bit nippy round the pipis!'

Kiwi Speak for, 'She's a bit cold out.' Pipis, a New Zealand shellfish, have no relevance whatsoever to the nether regions but it does rhyme pretty well, don't you think?

'Do you want me to get the wooden spoon?'

An intelligent ratbag would undoubtedly say no.
Sadly, however, most kids stand there waiting for another option.

'Had a fight with the lawnmower, mate?'

Unfortunately, some men always walk out of the barber looking
like Forrest Gump.

'Wouldn't that gap your shears?'

When Dad has just found out he no longer qualifies for the
Golden Oldies rugby side.

'You can watch *Survivor*, but as soon as the ABs start we're switching over.'

For the Kiwi dad, nothing is more sacred than watching his beloved All Blacks. Fans have been known to duck out of funerals and delay weddings to watch them. Note: not a good time (as my mother knows) to dust the TV screen.

'Get your A into G, you little toerag!'

The 'A' is otherwise known as your butt. The 'G' means 'gear'. Even though this sounds like a telling off, toerag is actually a term of endearment. The definition derives from old England where convicts used to tie bits of shirt around their toes and feet as a makeshift sock, hence 'toerag' means scoundrel, criminal or thief.

'Go and get me some ciggies from the dairy. I'll time ya.'

Extremely unlikely to be used nowadays, as you have to be 18 to buy smokes, but heard regularly when I was a nipper. Especially tempting when there was a Buzz Bar or Toffee Milk up for grabs.

'Sure you can go for a swim. But if you drown, don't come crying to me!'

Luckily Kiwi kids, like every ankle biter on the planet, have never understood sarcasm.

'Go and play in the traffic.'

'You're away with the fairies!'

'No *Fear Factor* on a school night!'

'No need to pack a sad.'

Don't be fooled by their age — Kiwi grandmas and grandads know exactly what's going on. Call them pop, call them nana — just don't call them late for breakfast. They don't miss a trick either, and have more sayings than you've had hot dinners. Many Kiwi 'nana-isms' as below, are a hangover from the British days.

'TTFN!'

Short for, 'Ta-ta for now,' although, much like the way 'Jack' is supposed to be short for 'John', it doesn't seem to save time for anyone!

'Toodle pip.'

An old-fashioned way of saying 'Spot you later.'

'Let's have some hymn hums.'

Nana Speak for a music jam (with piano, guitars, and comb and paper).

'Be back in two ticks, just going for a tinkle.'

Wouldn't you prefer hearing the above over, 'Going for a slash'?

'Just going for a wazz, won't be a jiffy. Back in two shakes of a lamb's tail.'

See above.

'Gordon Bennett! Who left my wireless out in the rain?'

There are many origins for the above, but there's no doubt the British comedies *Steptoe and Son* and *Only Fools and Horses* made the saying part of the New Zealand vernacular. As for the wireless? That's Grandad's transistor, which became a walkman, then an iPod.

'You couldn't see the road to the dunny if it had red flags on it!'

'Wherever you be, let your wind go free . . .'

'. . . for trying to hold it in will be the death of ye!' Well, this was true of my nana, anyway. Yours, like many others, may have opted for the alternative: 'Ladies should be polite and not ignite until out of sight.'

'It's the Asian invasion.'

About as un-PC as you can get, but still used by some grandparents. Alas, most people who use this phrase nowadays often pre-empt it with, 'Now, I'm not a racist, but . . .'

'Fill the flagon up while you're there.'

Aluminium cans are a grand invention but nothing beats the solid feel of an empty sherry flagon. There were stories in there, and jokes, and lies. And when it was empty you went and swapped it for a full one!

'Happy as Larry.'

The earliest printed reference to the above is from the New Zealand
writer G Meredith, dating from around 1875:
'We would be as happy as Larry if it were not for the rats.'

'Box of fluffies.'

Fluffy ducks are supposed to be cute. And I suppose a whole box of them
would make one feel warm and fuzzy. Ironically, the above saying is often
used in a sarcastic manner, as in, 'How ya feeling?' 'Box of fluffies.' Translation:
'Pretty shite, actually.' Nana, of course, wouldn't put it quite like that.

'Till the cows come home.'

Many believe this saying originated in 1829. At least, that's when it first
appeared in the *London Times* which ran the following story:
'If the Duke will but do what he unquestionably can do, and propose a Catholic
Bill with securities, he may be Minister "until the cows come home".'

'Were you born in a tent?'

I love the sarcasm in this saying — I can pretty much guarantee my nana knew I wasn't born in a tent but she still had the cheek to ask every time I forgot to close the lounge door. On that note, does anyone use those multicoloured home-knitted ridiculous-looking draught snakes anymore? Thought not.

'You make a better door than a window.'

After you've shut the door — and stopped whacking your sister with the draught snake — be sure not to stand in front of the telly while your gran's watching *Antiques Roadshow*.

'Fill 'er up at the bowser.'

Old-school name for the humble petrol pump.

'She's gone up north for a while.'

In the old days, people used to cover up a lot of stuff — like pregnancy. Incredibly, 'up north' must have been exactly the same distance and reason for going every time, as she always seemed to return nine months later.

In the old days a lot of New Zealand TV ads used to be better than the actual programmes. Maybe that's because we only had two channels. Actually, make that one — *Telethon* hogged one channel for nearly a week!

Either way, there was definitely less choice on the goggle box. Here are some sayings Kiwis learnt from the bits in between *Top Town* and *Spot On*.

'Relax, you're soaking in it!'

This was a Madgism. Madge was the hands and nails expert from the Palmolive ads. She was a bit of a know-it-all with an acerbic wit, advising women of the wondrous dishwashing liquid 'which softens hands while you do dishes!' Many of those early New Zealand ads came straight out of Australia. Even so, it may surprise some to know that Madge was actually an American actress. Jan Miner, from New York, appeared on and off Broadway from the 1940s to the 1980s. Without a doubt, though, she won most widespread attention as Madge, a character she played for 27 years. Jan Miner died in 2004, aged 86.

'One day, Roger Fitch, one day!'

The fat kid (Roger Fitch) gets the ice cream and the girl. Meanwhile, the blonde boy named Fay is left to pick up the pieces. The above became a catchphrase in New Zealand, literally translating to: 'You'll keep', 'I've got your number', or, 'I know the cut of your jib'.

'Ee, Ee, Brucie!'

Why we find irritating Aussies so endearing is anyone's guess. (Think Vince Martin) Maybe Brucie, who I believe was hawking cars, couldn't find any work in *Neighbours* or *The Sullivans*. As for Vince, he's surely a retread by now.

'We are the boys from down on the farm, we really know our cheese!'

Marketing genius. An ad that all Kiwis sang — all thanks to Ches and Dale.

'You can rock it, you can roll it! You can lock the rock and put your feet up. You can sit right back and really enjoy Your genuine La-Z-Boy!'

If you thought Ray Woolf was famous only for La-Z-Boy, think again. Most recently he appeared in *King Kong*. He once hosted his own TV show, starred on *Play School* and has even been on *Shortland Street*! It should be noted there are only nine New Zealanders who haven't been on *Shortland Street*.

'Go for G, G, G, G, G, G, G, G, Gerard! Go for Gerard and your roof is looking good!'

They say annoying jingles are the best because you remember them. In this case, add New Zealand's version of Engelbert Humperdinck, John Rowles, along with his young family — who just happen to be celebrating their new Gerard roof — and you have a song (?) that stuck to your brain like superglue. Though, to be honest, I never remember Rowles having such a pronounced stutter.

'You're not in Guatemala now, Dr Ropata.'

As soon as Temuera Morrison muttered this on New Zealand's longest-running soap, *Shortland Street*, it began life as a popular Kiwi saying.

Example:
'These pies aren't like the ones at my local!'
'You're not in Guatemala now, Dr Ropata.'

'Any . . . last requests?'

Walk up to anyone over the age of 30 and ask this. (Note: the pause is vital.)
A reply will be forthright, a hand expectant: 'Ah, Pixie Caramel.'

'Two all-beef patties, special sauce, lettuce, cheese, pickled onions on a sesame-seed bun!'

Once upon a time, when bad food wasn't bad for you, McDonald's
used to say if you could sing the above quickly enough they would give
you a free burger. If only schools had such incentives!

'Tiger, Tiger, Jelly Meat for dinner!'

The cat in question was eating what some Kiwis say used
to make up the contents of your average Georgie Pie.

'Life's a whole long journey, boy, before you grow too old, don't miss the opportunity to strike a little gold . . . Have a Crunchie, hokey pokey bar. Crazy Crunchie, hokey pokey bar!'

New Zealand's only train robbery — an advert for the still-popular Crunchie.

'Those were our people today. That's Holmes tonight.'

The nightly sign-off by TV host Paul Holmes. He's been on our screens for about 20 years and has endured scandals, *Dancing with the Stars*, and multiple aircraft crashes. He'll be remembered fondly for calling MP Tariana Turia a 'confused bag of lard', and former United Nations Secretary-General Kofi Annan a 'cheeky darkie' on his radio show.

There was absolutely *nothing* endearing about this Lots-a-Noodles ad.

'Trust British Paints . . .'

'. . . sure can!' Who doesn't still do the little drumroll on the paint can lid?
British Paints sure got their money's worth out of Rolf Harris,
who's now more famous for painting the Queen rather than the back fence.

'Where'd I get my bag? Lands for Bags of course!'

Some ads stick no matter how bad they are.
Then along comes some genius who takes the mickey out of it.
Case in point — Billy T James:
'Where'd I get my bag? I nicked it, eh!'

'I'll have an "O" for Awesome.'

Little did boxer David Tua know, after making this embarrassing slip on
Wheel Of Fortune, that it would be used colloquially all over the country,
not to mention printed on T-shirts and posters. Personally, I think David's right
— O for Oarsome is exactly how it should be spelt!

'Who stole the telly? Who stole the telly? Morris was very depressed!'

This was an NZI ad. Script: Cat chases parrot. Parrot gets so excited he knocks the cup off the kitchen sink. Then: 'They've paid! They've paid!' Stunning. Memorable. Or maybe I just remember it that way because I was six.

'If you drink and drive, you're a bloody idiot!'

The follow-up ad, sadly, never made it to the screen:
'Don't drink and drive; you might hit a bump and spill your drink.'

'It's the same day, David.'

Another ad in the drink-driving series. David, lying in bed with a smashed leg, having killed a couple of people in a car accident, is visited by his girlfriend. To rub salt into the wound, she brings in a speeding ticket and relays the news that he was doing 130 km minutes before the crash. (Note: 'Not a good time, love!')

'It's moments like these you need Minties!'

The Minties ad, ruthless in laughing at other people's misfortunes, was a truly memorable piece of television. Now, sadly, we're a little too PC to laugh at rugby players tripping over, or cricketers slipping on the proverbial banana skin.

'So Dad stopped the car, and Hugo said, "You go," but I said, "No, you go!" . . . Thank goodness for Kentucky Fried!'

Ah, the good old days, when they weren't afraid to tell us what the 'F' stood for.

'If it's not right, we'll put it right. And it is the putting right that counts.'

LV Martin and Son — 'and you won't be stuck with a lemon'.

'What's it going to be, Hokitika — the money or the bag?'

Small New Zealand towns came alive, all thanks to Selwyn Toogood.

'That messy trough should be a gone burger by the weekend.'

Like an old pair of jeans, TV One's weather presenter Jim Hickey has been with us through the highs and the lows. He retired and ran a cafe in New Plymouth then, thankfully, returned to our screens four years later.

'Keep cool till *After School*!'

Olly Olsen was the best thing on TV aside from *Flipper* and the Friday afternoon movie.

Jeff da Maori's sage words from *bro'Town*, New Zealand's
first local prime-time animated TV show.

SHOWER
SPEAKER

Kiwis can be a shy bunch. Unlike the Welsh, who burst into song at any rugby match, the average New Zealander generally doesn't sing (or dance for that matter) unless he's absolutely blottoed. Or he's in the safety of the shower. Here, then, are some Kiwi classics you may hear while waiting for the bathroom — if there's any hot water left.

'Da da da! Boom boom. Da da da. Boom boom.'

The first line to Dave Dobbyn's 'Slice of Heaven'. Difficult lyric to forget, even after a few. Dobbyn's band, DD Smash, were also responsible for another classic Kiwi saying, 'Cool Bananas'. the title of their 1982 record. Meaning 'choice', 'sweet' or 'rad', it is still widely used today.

'Victoooo-ria! What do you want from him, want from him?'

At the 2007 APRA Silver Scroll Awards, Jordan Luck (of The Exponents) was named as the first inductee to the New Zealand Music Hall of Fame. He deserves it. He's written some beaut songs — like the above.

'Ya . . . ya, ya, ya, ya . . . ya, ya, ya, ya! Forget about the last one, get yourself another!'

A line from a Dudes song, 'Bliss'. This would have to be New Zealand's quintessential Oktoberfest song. Oh, and how about, 'Aaaaa-sian cigarettes!'

'Poi E, whaka tata mai!'

In the 1980s, Dalvanius and the Patea Maori Club penned an anthem that made us all proud. Many a music fan taped the result off *RTR* or *Radio with Pictures*.

'Ba ba ba, ba baba ba, ba, ba ba baba ba!'

A show that had it all: dogs, sheep, and . . . that's about all. But who could forget *The Dog Show* theme?

'Pele preaches words of comfort Zina just hides her eyes Policeman taps his shades Is that a Chevy '69?'

How bizarre! When OMC (Otara Millionaires Club) penned this song, their name was ironic. But not for long. The tune became the biggest-selling New Zealand record of all time, going to #1 in New Zealand, Australia, Canada, Ireland, South Africa and Austria.

'Darlin', I'll say goodbye even though I'm blue, even though I'm blue, even though I'm blue!'

Another ditty by Jordan Luck and The Exponents. His website reports that, growing up, Jordan loved rugby, girls, netball and fish'n'chips at lunchtime. He also loved Sid Going, Pete Sinclair and the Oamaru Poultry Shows. And you don't get much more Kiwi than that.

'Dance, dance, dance to my ten guitars!'

I still can't work out whether it's a good or bad thing that Engelbert's song only really became a hit in New Zealand. Maybe we love dancing, or guitars, or crooners who describe themselves as 'Married — but available.'

'In a halfway house, halfway down Dominion Road!'

Don McGlashan is one of the few Muttonbirds who has (so far) avoided being eaten. Which is just as well really because he's a national treasure. Kiwis often wax lyrical over Number 8 wire, but Don can lay claim to the fact that he's the only muso in the world who has played a percussion instrument consisting of PVC piping struck with jandals! Rock on.

'How many dudes you know flow like this? Not many, if any!'

The catchphrase of 2002, thanks to Cantabrian rapper Scribe.

'There is no depression in New Zealand, there are no sheep on our faaa-arms!'

Sometimes described as New Zealand's alternative national anthem, the above was released in 1981, a perilous time in our country's history. A Muldoon government, rising unemployment, and fears that an impending Springbok rugby tour could cause massive civil unrest, were all perfect fodder for a bitingly cynical song dear to every Kiwi's heart.

'Cause it's you that I love, and it's true that I love, it's a love not given lightly!'

Chris Knox, originally from bands Toy Love and, later, Tall Dwarfs, is responsible for some of the best Kiwi song titles ever such as 'Fatty Fowl in Gravy Stew', 'Come in #52 — Your 15 Minutes Are Up' and 'The Second To Last Song Toy Love Wrote With Non Ad Lib Lyrics'. The above, 'Not Given Lightly,' was a love song written for his wife Barbara, and announced as New Zealand's thirteenth best song of all time, voted by APRA.

'Can't get enough, can't get enough, no!'

A crazy bunch of kids — Supergroove — had six top 10 hits during the 1990s. They were funky, rocky and crazy, and played shows, among other places, in South Africa, the UK, Finland, Sweden, Norway, Denmark and New York. From the top: 'Here it is for hers or his! For his, for hers, for better, for worse!'

'La da de da, la da de da, la da de da, la da de da!'

The Swingers began in New Zealand around June 1979. 'Counting the Beat' was recorded in August 1980, but a final mix didn't eventuate until late November. Its success was instant, going to #1 nationally within four weeks, and sales exceeded 100,000.

'Cheryl Mo-aaaa-na Marie!'

If Johnny Devlin was New Zealand's Elvis, John Rowles came a close second. All together now — 'Back home she's waiting for me!'

FARM
SPEAK

Righto, let's get them all out the way before we begin:

Did you hear the Kiwis have a new use for sheep? Meat and wool.

How do Kiwis find sheep in long grass?
Very nice, thank you very much.

A farmer's mate is having his way with a sheep in the barn back of beyond. Upon finding his friend, the farmer yells, 'Hey, you're supposed to be shearing that sheep!'
The response? 'You find your own bloody sheep!'

Okay. Can we continue? Good.

With 45 million sheep in New Zealand, the average Kiwi has to know what they're talking about on the farm, even if it means faking it. In this chapter are sayings for townies and cow cockies alike.

PS: Farmers (from anywhere) don't suffer fools gladly. Be sure to say the following in a confident, don't-mess-with-me tone.

PPS: This chapter is dedicated to my incredible Uncle Don and Aunty Margie, who have lived on a farm in Mangaweka for 45 years. Black singlet, two sausages for breakfast, as Kiwi as they come.

'Get in there, ya mongrel!' 'Get in behind!' 'Wayleggo!'

You'll hear the above yelled from paddocks in Pukekohe to the back blocks in Balclutha. It's generally directed at the dog with selective hearing and a wandering mind.

'He's all hat and no horse.'

Refers to the joker who's a talker, not a doer.

'The old Fergie's stuffed.'

On a farm it is common to refer not in general terms to the tractor — or the sheep, or even the woolshed — as a townie might. It's specifically the Fergie (short for tractor make Massey Ferguson) or the steel wheel.

'Poor thing's wool blind.'

The said sheep's wool has literally grown over its eyes.
As a result he doesn't see fences, opting instead to run straight into them.

'Blue's a bit whip-shy. If he doesn't play his cards right, there'll be no tucker.'

Blue is the dog that cowers or hides when the stock whip comes out.
Then again, what dog wouldn't?

'Barry's coming over later. He's an expert bum barber.'

Crutching is the process of cleaning dags from around a sheep's bum. And Barry the Bum Barber's the lucky guy to do it! Note: would you put that job title on your CV?

'It's colder than a witch's tit, wish I'd brought my bush nightie.'

It's hard to believe, but farmers get cold too. When the temperature drops —
and no-one's looking — the said Good Keen Bloke pulls on
his extra-long Swannie and makes a fresh hot cuppa char.

'He's a real Number-8 man.'

He's your go-to guy. Sometimes called a Swanndri man, or your Swannie bloke.

'You'll be pearl diving at the dag pickers' ball if you carry on like that!'

The farming equivalent of time out on the naughty step. The above applies to the
farm hand who has been relegated to the woolshed to sort the wool from the dags.

'Rattle your dags!'

Undoubtedly the most-used saying on the farm. Epitomised on the TV screen by Fred 'Kick it in the guts, Trev!' Dagg, but still used all over the show as a way to let stock know they need to get a move on. (Note for UK farmers: dingle berries and dags are the same thing, even if yours sound like something that should go with ice cream.) The above refers to the noise often made by the (dried) dags of scurrying, uncrutched sheep. 'Shake your shirt' (another Kiwi saying) will have a similar effect.

'Piss in your own time!'

This time Blue is taking a leak and admiring the view when he should be mustering for his master.

'Little bugger's gate shy!'

For the sheep that, for whatever reason, don't like the look of that gate! They baulk and hesitate, often needing a boot up the bum for desired effect.

'Don's taking up the burnt chops.'

Don is not, as you might imagine, scraping the charred remains from the barby, but is out mustering, bringing in the wool.

'These hockey sticks are a bit chewy. Must have been a tough old ewe.'

Some farm meat has the texture of bubble gum. These gristly, jaw-aching cuts are given the name 'hockey sticks'. Otherwise known as mutton chops or 365s.

'You're destined to become a pot licker, Smoke!'

For the farm dog who never leaves the couch, let alone the house.
Smoke will also be accused of being a 'powder puff' or a 'Sunday dog'.
The canine equivalent of a dole bludger.

'I'll have your guts for garters!'

The serial killers of the early 1800s would use the guts from their victims to make garters, which would then be sold at market stalls. Mental note for cows: don't piss off Serial Killer Farmer Guy.

'He's gained the bottom wire of the fence!'

The above refers to marrying the farmer's daughter, probably because it's the easiest part of the fence to make, as in, 'You shouldn't have too much trouble hooking up with her.' Though I don't know how the 'bottom wire of the fence' would feel about that!

'We need a new billy boy. Justin's as useless as tits on a bull.'

There's always a new kid in school. On the farm they're known as lambs, ewe lambs, gate-openers, remittance men or, as above, billy boys.

'He's had another brain fart.'

Refers to dogs, cattle and sheep who suddenly forget why they're on planet Earth, with unpredictable results.

'Just going to milk the girls over the backblocks.'

'Backblocks' is also used by Australians in reference to 'the back of beyond' and is often simply known in New Zealand as 'the bush'.
The 'girls' are the four-legged, uddered variety.

'Hold your horses!'

Literally translated, this means to keep your horse still. Slow things down, take your time. For example: 'Hold your horses, Gaz, you only just met her on the internet, and now you want to marry her!'

'What are ya? A Queen Street farmer?'

Hailing from the big smoke, the Queen Street farmer is the city businessman who, upon encountering a mid-life crisis, decides to buy some rural property.
It's fair to say he's not the most practical fella on the farm.
He doesn't favour getting his shoes dirty or getting up before 9am.
After all, he didn't move to the farm to work!

'Must be from north of the Bombays!'

Also affectionately known as 'Dorkland', New Zealand's biggest city (just north of the Bombay Hills) gets a bad rap for being just that. It happens everywhere around the world, mostly because we hate to see our big brother get too big for his boots.

'Get on the back or I'll give you the red smile!'

Things aren't about to end well for the animal on the receiving end of the above. Put simply, the 'red smile' is the result of a sharp instrument connecting with the neck. Hey, I never said farming was nice!

'He's been in the herringbone since sparrow's fart.'

The herringbone shed is named so because of the angle in which the (soon to be milked) cows are lined up. 'Sparrow's fart' means you should still be in bed.

PS2 may have taken over marbles, and sunhats may have become compulsory, but not a great deal has really changed in the Kiwi school yard. Kids still bludge coins for potato-top pies and scraps are still started over a box of Jaffas, though there are a few new phrases for the 21st century. Following are some that'll make you fit right in.

'I'll verse you at Pokemon.'

For some reason, kids nowadays 'verse' each other, instead of 'play against' or 'challenge'. Sure, it's not the Queen's English, but then nor is 'C U L8R OR 2MRW 4 A SK8!'

'Last one in's a sissy!'

You can 'bellyflop' or 'bomb' just don't be the last one in! And no running around the pool!

'That is so random!'

One for the new century. Once upon a time we would have said 'that's so left field'.

'Tahi, rua, toru, wha!'

Without exception, every song sung by a primary school teacher on guitar, started with these four words. It's Maori for 'one, two, three, four', if you've been living under a rock. Or are from Hawera. I can say that — I was born there!

'Tin a cocoa, tin a cocoa, cuppa Milo.'

Honky (Pakeha) version of the Maori welcome:
'Tena koutou, tena koutou, tena koutou, katoa.'

'Waipu? Cos you have to!'

Some New Zealand place names were surely written for kids.
Juveniles, okay most of my mates,
still laugh every time they drive past Waitomo ('white homo').

'Why can I live in Otaki?'

Purely coincidental that three neighbouring towns in the lower North Island, when said together, comprise a completely rational sentence: 'Waikanae Levin Otaki!'

'Ohau Manukau Levin Otaki?'

My workmate Jenny gave me this one, and it only just clicked: 'Oh, how many cow live in Otaki?'

'What do you get when you cross a cow, a sheep and a goat?'

'The Milky Baaa Kid!'

'Step on a crack, marry a rat!'

'Where's Maraetai?'

Just by my left eye.

'A...B...C...D...E...F ...G! Ha, ha, you have to marry Garry!'

Remember, as a kid, eating an apple? You twisted the stalk round and round and whatever letter you landed on, that's who you would marry? It never worked, of course. If you hated Garry, for example, you'd just give it a good yank on 'F'.

'Ah...ear...e...or...oo!'

The sound of 30 Kiwi school kids learning vowels in Maori.

'What did God say when he ate Fiji?'

'I want Samoa.'

'I know you are, you said you are, but what am I?'

Some things never change.

'Why don't you marry it then?'

Hard to fathom, I know, but I still use this corker, as in: 'I love the 'Naki.' 'Why don't you marry it then?' Sure, you get a look of disbelief — as in, 'Grow up!' — but trust me, it's worth it. Especially if there are kids around.

'Nine girls are running under a wharf and here I am.'

The Kiwi version of 'A red Indian thought he might eat toffee in church.' Which of course spells 'arithmetic'. Similarly, the above is an easy way to remember how to spell 'Ngaruawahia'.

'Wainuiomata where the boys are smarter. Paikakariki where the girls are sneaky.'

One for the Wellington kids.

'Far out, say it, don't spray it!'

Some kids get a little excited when they speak, often showering the recipient with half the Waikato River. If the above doesn't work, try 'I want the news, not the weather.' If that doesn't work, do what every 21st century family does: correspond only by text.

'Got any chuddy?'

Kiwi Speak for chewing gum.

'Giz a squiz at your answers.'

Cheating, Kiwi-style.

'Scrap! Scrap! Scrap!'

All good things must come to an end. The above, for example, is typically followed by the inevitable, slightly panicked squeal: 'Teacher's coming, teacher's coming!'

Take a deep breath: this may make you feel ancient. If you think Nomads, Treks and rat's tails still feature in School Speak, you'd better take your tube skirt and leg warmers back to 1985. That's more than 20 years ago!

Go on, admit it, you don't even know what a Year Six is!

Or what NCEA stands for! But let's move on before we feel any older. (It's 'National Certificate of Educational Achievement' in case you need it for Trivial Pursuit.)

'Here come the turds!'

Whoever coined this term, purely because it rhymed with 'third' former, deserves a cold Mello Yello.

'Wanna go round with me?'

Relationships were a lot simpler at primary school. Married to
Daniel Smithson by morning tea, divorced by woodwork,
and dating Joshua Ryan by lunch time. 'Wanna go round with me?'
was the junior equivalent of 'Can I buy you a drink?'

'Oh man, check out how many tags she's got on her nomads!'

In later life — when you become a manager — status is determined by
how many keys you have hanging from your belt, or where your name
features on the in-and-out whiteboard at reception. At school the coolest
guy always had at least 28 tags on his Nomads. Mystery and intrigue
surrounded this pigeon-toed god: how did he get them?
Who did he beat up to get them?
Only flags on your Chopper held more currency.

'O curry curry arna, I found a squashed banana!'

A parody of New Zealand's unofficial national anthem, 'Pokarekare Ana'. Well known to New Zealand school children.

'Got a spare 20c for spacies?'

Before Xbox, PlayStation, and Game Boy there was Space Invaders in the fish and chip shop. It was the size of a jukebox, with greasy joysticks. Kids from all over would ask the above (of just about anyone) if it meant they could 'clock it' before their pineapple fritters arrived.

'Oma rapeti, oma rapeti, Oma, oma, oma!'

Direct translation: 'Run rabbit, run rabbit, run, run, run!'

'One day a taniwha
Went swimming in the moana.
He whispered sweetly
in my taringa,
Won't you come along with me
There's such a lot to see
Underneath the deep
blue sea.'

In Maori mythology, taniwha are formidable creatures that
live in deep pools in rivers, dark caves or the sea.
Friendly creature then, to sing about at school!

'Cross-country tomorrow — are you gonna wag?'

Let's face it — cross-country and orienteering were built for madmen.
At school, anyone who didn't cheat — or nip home for lunch at the halfway mark —
was considered a freak. Wagging (Kiwi Speak for skipping school)
may have been a sounder option.

'Can I borrow some Twink? I've got black Vivid everywhere.'

The rest of the world calls it White Out; we call it Twink.
The rest of the world calls them markers; we call them 'Vivids'.

'Grouse, who gave you the hickey!'

When Shazza from third form came in with a golf ball-sized rash on her neck,
the rest of the class knew it wasn't from extreme vacuuming. Proof being that
Shane Butler was smiling like a loon during 'sustained silent reading'.

'Mr Bellamy's banned Bull Rush!'

Known in Britain as Bulldog, Bull Rush wasn't a game for the slow or weak. Indeed, it was a lunchtime activity characterised by its high level of violence and physicality. This is probably why it was banned. But hell we had a good time!

'Silent but violent, loud but proud!'

School, unlike the workplace, was the ideal place to make everybody aware of your bodily functions. Sigh. Why do we have to grow up?

'She's a minger.'

She would scare a bulldog off a meat truck. Face like a dropped pie. Whichever way you look at, the student in question isn't exactly an oil painting. Only a 'mole' is worse.

SATURDAY SPORTS SPEAK

Most Kiwi parents have one memory of Saturday mornings: driving their rug rats from netball games to rugby games to cricket matches. Then, in the middle of the week, from netball practice to cricket practice to rugby practice.

This ritual is as Kiwi as shark 'n' tatties on a Friday night. It's not uncommon for Chief Driver To All Events to quickly become Head Coach, Chief Washer Of Filthy Socks and Shouter of McDees should their team win.

Sadly, the sideline is often littered with parents who, despite their best intentions and obvious talent, never became All Blacks and Silver Ferns.

Speaking of which, it should be said that New Zealand's obsession for rugby is matched only by its dogged determination to put 'all', 'black' or 'silver' into every national team nickname. For example:

All Blacks (rugby),

All Whites (soccer),

Silver Ferns (netball),

Black Ferns (women's rugby),

Black Sticks (men's hockey),

Black Caps (cricket),

Tall Blacks (basketball),

Black Sox (softball),

Black Magic (America's Cup boat),

and Black Beauty (A1 race car).

This parochial naming of teams got a little out of hand a few years back when the New Zealand badminton team wanted to name themselves the, wait for it, Black Cocks. Certainly got the attention of those who thought the sport was boring! Anyway, I digress — back to the parents on the sideline . . .

'Oh, get off her!'

On the netball court, the player who is stuck to her opponent and
won't leave her alone is a prime target for this shout.
Could be followed up with, 'If she had a saddle, you could ride her!'

'Joshua, get onside!'

'Steven, you're all over the show!'

'Terence, don't dance with him, tackle him!'

'Jack, stick it up yer jumper and run!'

'Smash 'em into Tuesday, Stephanie!'

The ref at Saturday morning sport doesn't get paid — but does get abuse. These are a few you shouldn't use from the sideline:

'Wakey, wakey, touch judge!'

'I'm blind, I'm deaf, I wanna be a ref!'

'Move around, ref, that patch of grass hasn't seen the sun for 20 minutes!'

'Do you want a harmonica instead of that whistle, ref?'

'Come on, ref, are your eyes painted on?'

'I pee straighter than that, ref!'

'If that's 10 metres, ref, I would like you to fit me a carpet!'

Alas, when the kids leave the pitch and the big boys
take over the real fun starts:

'Show 'im a clean pair of heels!'

'You couldn't pass wind!'

'You couldn't pass a kidney stone!'

'Run it like you stole it!'

'Your mum rang to say your bath is ready!'

'You couldn't score in a brothel!'

'Bring out the screens!'

Thanks to Graham from the Auckland Rugby Union Supporters Club for this last one. In the old days, when a racehorse broke its leg on the track the owner would bring out a big screen, behind which the horse would be put down. Rugby fans have adopted it and will yell it out when their least-favourite player goes down.

HORSE-RACING SPEAK

Rugby, racing and beer — a recipe for Kiwi leisure. With its temperate climate, rich pastures and plentiful sunshine, Aotearoa has always been a pretty good place to jump on a horse. Race meets became a feature of the first anniversary celebrations in Wellington, Auckland, Nelson, Otago and Canterbury. The first ones were probably held around 1840 by the military garrison at Auckland.

Fast forward about 170 years and there are a few things you need to know before you head down to the track: remember to load your pockets with dosh, wear a poncy hat (and that goes for the ladies too) and have a flutter on the trifecta, quinella, superfecta or exacta! Just be sure to read the following before you make a foal of yourself.

Poor puns aside, here's some jargon to get you through the Saturday meet.

'Bet until your nose bleeds.'

In racing terms, it's a 'dead cert' and punters should keep betting unless they become physically incapacitated.

'She's paying big bikkies.'

Superwines, Ginger Nuts and Mallowpuffs are the biscuits of choice in New Zealand. The bikkies for offer at the race track, however, will go a lot further than what you dunk in your morning cuppa.

'Trust me to pick a chaff burner.'

Some people, me included, never win the meat pack down at the pub. Similarly, if I was to back a horse, I'd probably pick the one slower than a week of Sundays.

'Have a yarn to the asparagus.'

At the track, it's best to stick with the bloke who's done his homework. In horse-racing terms, that fount of knowledge resembles the spear-headed vegetable, as in 'more tips than a tin of asparagus'.

'You know what Stan's like; cuts his own hair.'

In the pub, he's the Scotsman. At the track, he's the punter who is extremely tight with his hard-earned coin.

'Here comes Cyril, he's such a bloody emu.'

Like a bum rummaging through bins for a meal, the 'emu' is the person who picks up discarded betting tickets on a racecourse, hoping that some will pay for his taxi ride home. This opportunist closely resembles Australia's largest native bird when feeding.

'They're getting up without names today.'

It's always a good day when the underdog wins. Indeed, that's probably why we follow sport. You'll hear the above at the course if a number of long shots have achieved the impossible.

'It'll pay the grandstand.'

Likely to be muttered when one or more outsiders win or run a place. The punter in question, unable to believe his luck, will no doubt follow the above quote with 'The Milky Bars are on me!'

'Better call the TAB, boy.'

Not many punters call it the Totalisator Agency Board,
but a lot of Kiwis do call it!

'I wouldn't back it with bad money.'

Keep those mitts in your pockets. Or go and get another bag of chips.

'One Easy Bet thanks, mate.'

Some Kiwis throw their money at the pokies. Others like a scratchie at the dairy. An Easy Bet is when you fling your fiver over and let the one-sided, conniving computer pick your fate.

'Lucky I backed a mudlark!'

You have to know your horses, but you also have to know the conditions. The above refers to the bolter that goes well on a wet track.

Ah, the Kiwi pub. The Patea Maori Club on the jukebox and Speight's on tap. The sound of the perfect pool break and girls dancing around their handbags. Here's language you'll hear from the dartboard to the dunny.

'Maaaaaate!'

Many uses:

1. Hello.
2. Gidday.
3. Must be your shout.

'Are you unders or overs?'

No pub in New Zealand is complete without a pool table. Overseas, the balls are known as 'stripes and solids'. Here they're 'unders and overs'. And, whatever you do, don't sink the black off the break.

'Skull! Skull! Skull!'

The above is normally yelled during the heinous act of consuming
(on your 21st) what is commonly referred to as a 'yardy'.
'Skull' is probably a variation of 'skol', a Scandinavian toast.

'How about a Waitakere Dakiri?'

In West Auckland, where the footwear of choice is ug boots (sheepskin boots)
and family fights are started if someone from a Holden family buys a Ford, the
Waitakere Dakiri (bourbon and Coke) is a popular mid-morning beverage.

'Eating's cheating!'

A saying no doubt responsible for New Zealand's binge-drinking epidemic. Sadly, when you're in your late teens there's no such thing as good food and good wine. In fact, quite the opposite: a good chuck makes room for more beer.

'Got gorse in your pocket?'

Also dubbed the 'Aussie haka'. The bloke who never shouts, always heading to the bog when it's his round. 'Got katipos in your pockets?' can also be used.

'Can you believe this place hasn't got EFTPOS?'

Everyone remembers their flatting days when being 'declined' was a common occurrence. Normally, it must be said, it was when you'd just ordered three rounds of tequila, a couple of chasers and five packs of salt and vinegar chips. For the most part, the electronic funds transfer at point of sale is a great invention, although a little dangerous if you have a tendency to always shout the lads.

'Got any moolah for ciggies?'

'You got any spare pingers for fags?' works just as well.
Or you could just spend your beer money on nicotine patches.

'If the mobile boxing doesn't finish soon, my Mrs will be ropeable.'

Translation: If the rugby league doesn't finish soon my wife
will have a noose ready for me.

'Don't break the seal, bro.'

The fine art of holding off going to the loo as long as possible.
The theory is that once you start, you won't stop.

'Wank you very crutch.'

Another annoying one from those people who can't help saying,
'Step into my orifice.'

'My round. You get the first one at the Cake Tin.'

Very shifty move by the buyer. Drinks at Wellington's stadium — known as the
Cake Tin due to its distinctive shape — will cost an arm and a leg.

'Got any electric puha?'

Otherwise known as 'dack', 'Bob Marleys' or 'Northland ciggies'. Whatever the
name, expect to be asked to detour via Burger King on the way home.

'FMBs at two o'clock.'

Some people have a way with words. Whoever came up with 'F*** me boots'
surely deserves some sort of literary award. A Whitcoulls voucher at least.

'Piker, he's having an L&P!'

The drink Lemon & Paeroa, world famous in New Zealand, is fine with a splash of Southern Comfort. But if you get caught drinking it straight — and the rest of your mates have spent the evening working on a hangover of Jonah Lomu proportions — look out!

'You'd think he'd give us mate's rates.'

Not much point having a friend behind the bar if he doesn't pass on his staff discount.

'What do you want to go and live with those sheep stealers for?'

Former prime minister Rob Muldoon once said, 'New Zealanders who emigrate to Australia raise the IQ of both countries.' Still, if a Kiwi really wants to go and live with a bunch of sheep rustlers there's not a lot you can do.

'He's on his OE, earning big bikkies in London now.'

The big OE or 'overseas experience', as it is commonly known, is a ritual for many Kiwis. Typically, it involves visiting 23 European countries in 18 days but not leaving the bar in each one. It also involves earning £3 an hour (that's about $9) in a grotty East London pub, sleeping under the stairs in a Willesden Green flat and going to The Church to complain about how much the Tube is. Sometimes though, it must be said, 'big bikkies' can be made if the right job is found. Then the OE never ends and Mrs Birch from Matamata only sees her son every second Christmas.

'That sheila just gave me the evils. Guess we won't be bumping uglies tonight.'

Self-explanatory. I'd rather not go into details.

'Mutton dressed as lamb.'

Could there be a more apt Kiwi saying? As if you didn't know, it refers to a middle-aged or elderly person trying to look younger.

'Typical scarfie — always on the turps.'

Local nickname for Otago University students, due to the extreme cold of the south. By God they can drink; some of them can even study.

'Best get on the shicker express.'

Back in the days of the six o'clock swill, when men from all over the country would guzzle as much beer as they could before closing time, the shicker express, as it was known, was the first train, tram or bus to leave. It was named as such because you were normally 'shickered' when you got on it! The word 'shicker' is actually an adaptation of Yiddish 'shiker', ironically the surname of one of my mates. Always wondered why he enjoyed a pint.

'You're taking me on a tiki tour.'

Directed at the taxi driver who thinks he can take the long way home just because it's the end of the night and you happen to be utterly plastered. And why not? What you should be worried about is the $100 soiling fee.

STR⌀PPY
SPEAK

It takes a lot to make a Kiwi lose their rag. A loss by the All Blacks will do it. Or being accused of being Australian. Generally, though, most Kiwis don't do their na-na unless they really have to.

Some would also venture to say Kiwis never have an opinion. That may be because Kiwis don't like to rock the boat, or cause grief for the sake of it. And although the joke 'Why did the Canadian cross the road? To get to the middle' could also apply to Aotearoa, it would be unfair to claim Kiwis don't know how to start a bun fight when need be.

It's most surprising then, given that most Kiwis are placid, unflappable types, the number of ways in which Kiwis do lose their rag. The following are muttered and spluttered from dairies in Dannevirke to malls in Mangere.

'SHUDDUP!'

Inspired by the one and only *Footrot Flats* cartoon.
Why use two words when one does the job?

'Get stuffed.'

Usual response by any Kiwi when it's suggested his homeland
is a seventh state of Australia.

'Get out of it!'

When your mate is about to take the last Snifter from the box.

'Bully for you.'

Typically muttered to a Kiwi workmate who has just received a pay rise,
car park and free trip to Rarotonga. Tall Poppy Syndrome at its finest.
'Whoopdee shit' also works just fine.

'Blimmin 'eck!'

A Kiwi's reaction to getting five numbers in Lotto.

'Blow me down!'

Same Kiwi getting six numbers!

'Spare me days!'

Realising it was last week's ticket.

'Bite your bum!'

Consider this a personal dedication to my Nana Noeline who always used to say this. It's not surprising given that her younger sister, Margie, used to curse, 'Poopy fart shit!'

'Meathead!'

Said to the Kiwi who fills his new petrol Mitsi with diesel.

'Dipstick!'

For the Kiwi who filled his diesel with 91.

'Don't get toey.'

In Aussie slang, 'toey' means 'sexually aroused'.
The same word in New Zealand means 'agitated' or 'annoyed'.
The image originated with horses on alert,
toeing the ground with a hoof.
Note: whether they were slightly annoyed —
or sexually excited — is still unclear.

'Sorry, mate, you're shit out of luck.'

Can be heard muttered at barbies, by the person who's
secured the last beer from the chilly bin.

'Don't throw a hissy fit!'

Said to the Kiwi wife who's just been informed by her husband that he'd rather
clean the toilet than stay another week with the rellies. Also known as a 'wobbly'.

'Geez Wayne, you've got the brains of a chocolate fish!'

What a Kiwi says to his mate
upon discovering he's running for
the McGillicuddy Serious Party.

'Keep yer shirt on!'

'Get off the grass!'

'Oh, bull pucky!'

'Bloody drongo,
hori poofter.'

'You wouldn't know
shit from clay!'

'No need to spit the dummy.'

'You've got the brains of a retarded whitebait!'

'You couldn't organise a piss-up in a brewery.'

'Don't have an epi.'

Kiwi drivers are among the worst in the world. Think, if you will, of that classic Disney skit in which Goofy — laid back, warm, friendly, couldn't-do-enough-for-you Goofy — gets behind the wheel and instantly transforms into a homicidal maniac.

Kiwis don't know the meaning of 'merge'. They consider you a sissy if you let someone (anyone!) pass. And they have a colourful repertoire of sayings especially reserved for the confines of the Corolla.

'Did you get a horn for Christmas?'

Shouted at a driver with a lead hand.

'Do you think you own the road?'

A classic.

you loser!'

Some Kiwis don't turn their indicators off. Some don't even know they exist.
Yell this at the driver who thinks we're mind readers.

'Where'd you get your licence — a Weetbix packet?'

Most Kiwis remember, as kids, fishing around in the Weetbix packet for the latest promotional toy. (There had to be some incentive in healthy eating.) But kids aren't dumb. Indeed, most throw their grubby mitts straight to the treasure and feed the remainder of the contents to the dog. The above is often yelled at a driver who clearly hasn't gained his licence the traditional way.

'Drive it or sell it!'

Muttered to the rich ponce in the Merc who doesn't know his clutch from his accelerator.

'Check out the drongo in the Mazda-bator.'

There was a time in New Zealand when every car had to be a Ford or a Holden. Somewhere along the way the cheaper, sportier Japanese imports arrived. They were flashy, showy and seemed to be made of tin, and the above is an example of what your average V8 fan thought of them.

'Come on, it's not getting any greener!'

Bellowed at the driver who is lighting a ciggie, texting his mates and shaving when he's supposed to be moving forward. To make matters worse, this driver will panic and stall when he finally realises the lights have changed.

'It's in good nick, got a WOF last month.'

By no means is this an indication that the car in question comes with its own canine. WOF is short for Warrant of Fitness. Every car needs one; that's not to say every car has one.

'It's just a small ding.'

What the 16-year-old says to the car's owner when he
hits the pine tree in the driveway.

'What a rust bucket!
That old bomb shouldn't
even be on the road!'

This car hasn't seen a WOF in years.

'You can take it for a blat,
just don't prang it.'

The dictionary definition of 'blat' is 'to make a loud or raucous noise'.
In this case, however, 'blat' means taking the car in question for a spin.
And 'don't prang it' means 'If you're going to take it for a test drive,
don't hit the pine tree in the driveway.'

'Blimmin boy racers!'

Yelled by the over-75s.

'Bloody Sunday drivers!'

Yelled by the under-25s.

'Crash hot!'

'For real?'

'Primo!'

'What's the happs?'

'Too much!'

'That's sick!'

'Oh, true?'

'It's going off!'

'Oh, stink, bro!'

'Choice!'

'Sup?'

'Chur.'

'How many were there? Untold.'

'Don't have a mental.'

'Statue, bro?'

Correct answer to — what did one Maori statue say to the other Maori statue?
More commonly used when two people meet on a pitch-black night.

'Bruce's moved from A-von-da-lay to Papa-two-toes.'

Just as Mrs Bucket on *Keeping Up Appearances* preferred to be known as
'Mrs Bouquet', so too do folk in Avondale and Papatoetoe prefer a
more upmarket nickname for their suburbs.

'It was mint! I got it from the Ware Whare.'

Getting a bargain at The Warehouse.

THINGS YOU'LL NEVER HEAR A SELF-RESPECTING KIWI MALE SAY

'Let's think big.'

'I don't mind if Australia wins this one.'

'Shall we leave a tip?'

'Russell Coutts is still a full-blooded Kiwi in my books.'

'I'll have a shandy.'

'Let me tell you how to get to my favourite fishing spot.'

'We're heading to Invercargill for the summer.'

'Do you like my Stubbies? I got them from Warnocks.'

'Make mine a Rheineck.'

'I won't have a pie —
bad for the blood pressure.'

'I'll just have an instant.'

'I'll have another
piece of quiche!'

'I should
finish reading
*The Penguin History
of New Zealand*
this week.'

'I totally understand
NCEA.'

'We need someone like Muldoon in charge again.'

'I think I'll do some study instead of playing touch tonight.'

'Great, they've got shrimp cocktails!'

'I'm going to hire someone to mow my lawns.'

Dedication

Thanks a ton to the following: my wondrous wife
Amy, CJ and LA Brown ('I can't do a thing with my hair —
it's all over my head'), my late Nana Noeline and Nana Marg,
Rachael Lee (Peanut trees and Pickled Bums), Colin Nichols,
Esther Malcolm, Margie McCord, Victoria University Press,
Jacqui Donaldson, Jenny Fromen, Jenny-May Coffin,
The Godzone Dictionary by Max Cryer, *A Dictionary of Modern
New Zealand Slang* edited by Harry Orsman, folksong.org.nz,
The Road to Castle Hill by Christine Fernyhough, Yvonne Koolis
from Universal Music Publishing, Paul McLaney from Mushroom
Music New Zealand, Patricia Ngawera from the Patea Maori Club,
Ian Morris, Dave Dobbyn, Jordan Luck, Scribe, the Swingers,
Supergroove, Chris Knox and anyone else who helped,
yeah, nah, yeah, nah . . .

If you have any Kiwi sayings you'd like to share,
please email them to sayings@rugbyspeak.com
for possible inclusion in future editions.